THE ART OF FINANCIAL CLARITY

A SIMPLIFIED GUIDE TO DOUBLE ENTRY ACCOUNTING

DAVID RUDDER

ISBN: 979-8-9891633-0-4

CONTENTS

Introduction   i

1   Double Entry Accounting Chart   1

2   Balanced Financial Records   3

3   General Ledger Accounts   7

4   Recording Financial Transactions   18

5   Financial Reports   23

6   Summary   26

About the Author   27

INTRODUCTION

One evening my thoughts wandered back to my bookkeeping class, several decades ago, as a junior in high school. After reading the first two chapters of the textbook, the subject resonated with me. The next year, I decided accounting would be my vocation. As my thoughts continued, I wanted to capture the big picture of double entry accounting in one chart. At the time, I didn't have any intention of doing anything with it. I completed the chart and after two weeks, I made enhancements. Two weeks after that, I made additional changes. Then I thought, if I were to write an accounting book, I would write about the conceptual basis of double entry accounting. A week later, I started writing.

This is a short book focused on the conceptual basis and the basic mechanics and application of accounting. Double entry accounting is the foundation of every accounting system. The chart is displayed in the first chapter. The book's content is useful for anyone that wants to learn the basis of accounting. Specifically, this will help persons thinking about studying accounting to solidify the interest. This will help business students get a head start for the required accounting class. Accounting teachers can use this book as supplementary material for their classes.

1. DOUBLE ENTRY ACCOUNTING CHART

The following chart illustrates all the conceptual elements of double entry accounting. It will help to give yourself a few minutes to review and absorb the big picture in the chart. Double entry accounting is an eloquent and intricate application of the simple math equation c = a + b.

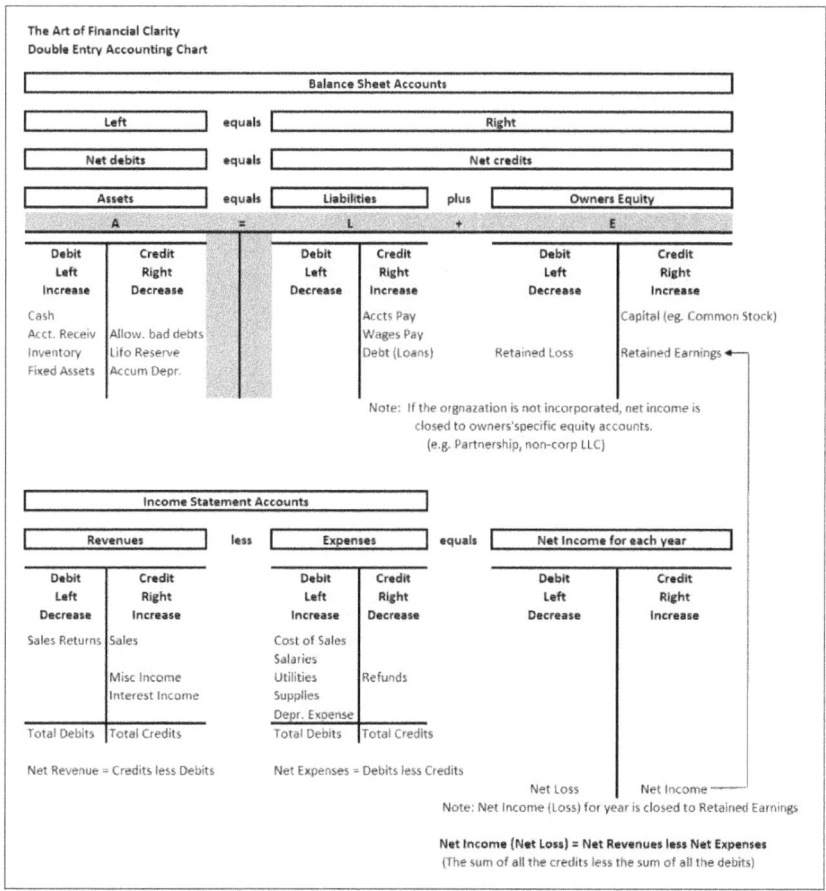

The Art of Financial Clarity
Double Entry Accounting Chart

Balance Sheet Accounts						

Left	equals	Right			

Net debits	equals	Net credits			

Assets	equals	Liabilities	plus	Owners Equity	
A	**=**	**L**	**+**	**E**	

Debit	Credit		Debit	Credit		Debit	Credit
Left	Right		Left	Right		Left	Right
Increase	Decrease		Decrease	Increase		Decrease	Increase
Cash				Accts Pay			Capital (eg. Common Stock)
Acct. Receiv	Allow. bad debts			Wages Pay			
Inventory	Lifo Reserve			Debt (Loans)		Retained Loss	Retained Earnings
Fixed Assets	Accum Depr.						

Note: If the orgnazation is not incorporated, net income is
closed to owners' specific equity accounts.
(e.g. Partnership, non-corp LLC)

Income Statement Accounts					

Revenues	less	Expenses	equals	Net Income for each year	

Debit	Credit		Debit	Credit		Debit	Credit
Left	Right		Left	Right		Left	Right
Decrease	Increase		Increase	Decrease		Decrease	Increase
Sales Returns	Sales		Cost of Sales				
			Salaries				
	Misc Income		Utilities	Refunds			
	Interest Income		Supplies				
			Depr. Expense				
Total Debits	Total Credits		Total Debits	Total Credits			
Net Revenue = Credits less Debits			Net Expenses = Debits less Credits				

Net Loss | Net Income
Note: Net Income (Loss) for year is closed to Retained Earnings

Net Income (Net Loss) = Net Revenues less Net Expenses
(The sum of all the credits less the sum of all the debits)

Going forward, the use of the word "accounting" refers to double entry accounting. All modern accounting systems are double entry accounting systems.

Accounting systems have the following elements:

> Balanced financial records that follow the two accounting rules. The two rules are the accounting equation that states "Assets equal Liabilities plus Owners' Equity", and transactions have two sides that are equal, that is "Debits equal Credits". These two rules state the inherent nature of the basic math equation $c = a + b$.

> A system of accounts to categorize and record financial transactions that facilitate reporting financial results of an organization.

> Methods, procedures, and mechanics for recording financial transactions in the accounts.

> Reporting financial results. Reports are generated periodically (monthly, quarterly, yearly) from the balances in the accounts. The primary financial reports are a balance sheet, income statement, and cash flow statement. However, there are additional reports that organizations generate for internal information needs, regulatory reporting, for decision support, and any other information that may be needed.

Modern accounting systems are computer software driven. An accounting system might be a stand-alone software program or might be part of an enterprise-wide software application. The financial reporting aspect of an accounting system is usually a separate software program from the system of accounts aspect of the software. All accounting systems contain the conceptual elements.

Now that we have the big picture of the conceptual elements of an accounting system, let's explore each element.

2. BALANCED FINANCIAL RECORDS

Accounting is an eloquent and intricate application of the simple math equation $c = a + b$. There are two conceptual rules in accounting. The first rule is the accounting equation, stated as "Assets equals Liabilities plus Owners' Equity". The second rule is that transactions have two sides, a left side and a right side; in accounting terminology this rule is stated as "Debits equal Credits". In addition, the sum of all the transactions debits equals the sum of all the transactions credits. The two rules state the inherent nature of the basic math equation of $c = a + b$. The accounting equation of $A(Assets) = L(Liabilities) + E(Owners' Equity)$ is a financial version of that simple math equation.

Accounting Mechanics

Let's explore the mechanics of accounting. At a detailed level, each transaction follows the two rules.

> ➤ A financial transaction can increase one thing on the left side (Assets) and decrease another thing on the left side (Assets). For example, plus A1 minus A2.

> ➤ A financial transaction can increase one thing on the left side (Assets) and increase one thing on the right side (Liabilities or Owners Equity). For example, plus A1 = plus L1; or plus A1 = plus E1.

> ➤ A financial transaction can increase one thing on the right side (Liabilities or Owners Equity) and decrease another thing on the right side (Liabilities or Owners Equity). For example, plus L1 minus L2 or plus L1 minus E1.

> ➤ A financial transaction can decrease one thing on the left side (Assets) and decrease one thing on the right side (Liabilities or Owners Equity). For example, minus A1 = minus L1.

> ➤ Any transaction can have multiple components. There can be multiple accounts increased or decreased (not limited to

3

two). The key is the two rules need to be followed; A = L + E and the debits (sum of the left side) needs to equal the credits (sum of the right side).

In accounting terminology, all this "lefting" and "righting" of transactions are called "debiting" and "crediting". The words "debit" and "credit" are also used as verbs. For example, instead of saying, "I am going to make an entry to the left side of the accounts payable account", accountants say "I am going to debit accounts payable". Likewise, instead of saying "I am going to make an entry to the right side of the cash account", accountants say "I am going to credit cash". It is clear now that in accounting the word "debit" simply means left and the word "credit" simply means right.

As a side note, for practical reasons in spreadsheets and in accounting software, a debit is often represented as a positive number and a credit is often represented as a negative number.

More about Debits and Credits.

As stated above a transaction can increase or decrease an asset (left side of equation). A transaction can increase or decrease a liability or equity or both (right side of equation).

> ➤ Remember in accounting debit means left and credit means right.

> ➤ Remember the accounting equation is A (Assets) = L (Liabilities) + E (Equity).

> ➤ Remember in accounting debits equal credits.

A transaction can increase or decrease an asset (left side of equation). Is an increase in an asset a debit or credit? Is a decrease in an asset a debit or credit?

> ➤ An increase in an asset (left side of equation) is a debit (left).

> ➤ A decrease in an asset (left side of equation) is a credit (right).

> ➤ What? But assets are on the left side of the equation. Yes, they are. Let's ask ourself, when we decrease an asset (the opposite

of an increase), that is a negative on the left side. And the opposite of left is right. Therefore, a negative on the left side is a credit.

A transaction can increase or decrease a liability (right side of equation). Is an increase in a liability a debit or credit? Is a decrease in a liability a debit or credit?

> An increase in a liability (right side of equation) is a credit (right).

> A decrease in a liability (right side of equation) is a debit (left).

> What? But liabilities are on the right side of the equation. Yes, they are. Let's ask ourself, when we decrease a liability (the opposite of an increase), that is a negative on the right side. And the opposite of right is left. Therefore, a negative on the right side is a debit.

A transaction can increase or decrease equity (right side of equation). Is an increase in equity a debit or credit? Is a decrease in equity a debit or credit? Transactions to equity accounts follow the same pattern as liability accounts since equity is on the right side of the equation.

Debit and Credit Dynamics using Accounting Equation

The debit and credit dynamics can be illustrated in the accounting equation. Below is the example of decreasing an asset and decreasing a liability.

> A(original) minus A(1) equals L(original) minus L(1) plus E(original).

> Using basic algebra, we can display the equation as A(original) plus L(1) equals L(original) plus A(1) plus E(original). This simply moves all the debits to the left of the equal sign and all the credits to the right of the equal sign.

> This example shows the two accounting rules in action, $A = L + E$, and debits = credits.

A note about technology. Regardless of the technology used, whether on paper or computer software systems, all accounting systems follow the accounting rules. Before computers, it was a handwritten process on paper. There were companies that developed and sold pre-printed accounting forms and paper systems that streamlined the process. When computers and the related software emerged, accounting systems went digital. With the automation, in modern accounting systems, on some data entry screens, only one side of the entry is input and shown. In those scenarios, the other side of the entry is done automatically by the software, behind the scenes.

With the conceptual understanding of accounting, and the general mechanical understanding in applying the principles, we need a system of accounts to record transactions. The major component of the account system is called the "General Ledger" and the accounts in the general ledger are called "General Ledger Accounts".

3. GENERAL LEDGER ACCOUNTS

There are many types of accounts. There are customer specific accounts, vendor specific accounts, product record specific accounts, fixed asset record accounts, and there are the general ledger accounts. This book's focus is on the general ledger accounts.

The purpose of the general ledger accounts is to record financial transactions in a way that facilitate reporting of financial balances and transactions.

> ➤ Remember the major categories in the accounting equation, Assets, Liabilities, Owners Equity and that $A = L + E$.

> ➤ Conceptually, there could be three general ledger accounts. There could be one general ledger account called "Assets", one general ledger account "Liabilities" and one general ledger account called "Owners' Equity". However, only having three accounts is not useful or practical.

Going forward, when you see the word "account" by itself, it refers to a general ledger account. If a different type of account is intended, vendor account for example, the account type will be explicitly stated.

There are numerous reasons why organizations need to have more than three accounts (general ledger accounts). A few reasons are:

> ➤ For internal management purposes, organizations need to know and report the types of assets it has and the types of liabilities it owes, and the components of owners' equity.

> ➤ For regulatory purposes, data needs to be gathered for filings, in a reasonable amount of time, for example, income taxes.

> ➤ In the United States, public corporations need to produce information for SEC (Securities and Exchange Commission) reporting to the federal government.

The general ledger accounts are the primary repository for financial transactions and balances. This facilitates the financial reporting of an organization.

As a side note, for the same reasons as the need for financial information, there are many types of information an organization needs to capture, monitor, and report, in addition to the financial balances and activity contained in the general ledger accounts.

Let's explore the assets component of the accounting equation.

Assets

Generally, assets are things an organization owns, has possession of, have the rights to use, or future rights to obtain or use. Some common examples are cash, accounts receivable, credit card receivable, inventory, fixed assets, and financial investments.

There are many types of assets that need to be tracked and reported, both for internal and external purposes. To illustrate the application for accounting, I will describe the basic accounting mechanics for three common types of assets; cash, accounts receivable, and fixed assets. In addition to general ledger accounts previously introduced, with accounts receivable and fixed assets, the concepts of the "subsidiary ledger" and the "contra-account" are introduced.

Cash

Now let's focus on cash. An organization can have several bank accounts for different purposes. There might be one bank account for funding payroll, another bank account for operating expenses, and another bank account for deposits from customers or credit card companies.

➤ In principle, in the general ledger, there could be one account called "Cash" to record all the activity from all the bank accounts. It would be very challenging to reconcile the bank accounts each month if there was only one cash account in the general ledger.

➤ It is prudent and common to reconcile every bank account every month. Therefore, to make that easier, it is helpful and practical to have a separate general ledger account for each bank account.

Accounts Receivable

Another common asset account is an account for accounts receivable. A company may allow customers a few days or weeks to pay when a sale is made. Therefore, an account is needed to record those transactions. If an organization has numerous customers that are allowed to pay days or weeks later, there is a need to know what each customer owes, and to record other information for each customer.

➢ Conceptually, there could be a separate general ledger account for each customer. However, that is not useful or practical.

➢ The primary purpose of the general ledger is to categorize activity in enough detail to facilitate and support financial reporting for the purposes described earlier in the book. One account for accounts receivable activity serves the purpose of a general ledger account.

➢ To manage and run the business, though, an organization also needs to have records for each customer to monitor balances, past due amounts, and to respond to customer questions. This introduces the concept of the "subsidiary ledger". Specifically, for accounts receivable, the "Accounts Receivable" subsidiary ledger". In an accounts receivable subsidiary ledger, there is an account for each customer, that is, a "customer account". At any point in time, the sum of all the customer balances in the "Accounts Receivable" subsidiary ledger equals the balance in the "Accounts Receivable" general ledger account.

➢ Before computers, when accounting records were on paper, subsidiary ledgers were separate ledger books from the general ledger book. On modern accounting software systems, subsidiary ledger data might be a separate module; or part of an integrated database system. Regardless, the end user usually navigates to a separate screen to view subsidiary ledger data.

Fixed Assets

Another common asset type is "Fixed Assets". Each organization decides the specific general ledger accounts they need for each account type. For example, for fixed assets, there is usually an account for furniture and fixtures, an account for equipment, and an account for buildings if the buildings are owned. If buildings are leased, there is an account for leasehold improvements. Usually, there is also a subsidiary ledger for fixed asset accounts. In a fixed asset subsidiary ledger, each fixed asset, the CFO's office desk, for example, has its own "fixed asset" account, which is called a "fixed asset record". When a subsidiary ledger represents things, the account for each thing is called a "record" instead of an account.

Contra-accounts

An asset type can also have a "contra-account". A "contra-account" is used when there are two distinct types of transactions for an asset type that need to be recorded into two separate accounts. Two common examples of a contra-account are "allowance for bad debts" for accounts receivable and "accumulated depreciation" for fixed assets.

Allowance for Bad Debts

Earlier, "Accounts Receivable" was introduced. Generally, businesses sell goods and services to customers and receive payments from customers.

➢ In business, sometimes a few customers fail to pay the balances owed. In those situations, after collection efforts are exhausted, the customer balance is usually written-off.

➢ Businesses won't know which customers will fail to pay. Therefore, it is necessary to estimate at the end of an accounting time-frame the amount of the accounts receivable balance that will eventually be written off.

➢ The estimated future bad debt amount is booked (credited) to the allowance for bad debts account and bad debt expense is debited. I will say more about revenues and expenses later in the book.

➢ Once it is known that a particular customer is not going to pay what is owed, to write-off the customer balance, the general ledger entry is to debit "allowance for bad debts" and credit "accounts receivable". And the particular customer account is credited in the accounts receivable subsidiary ledger.

➢ The net accounts receivable balance is the balance in the "Accounts Receivable" account less the balance in the

"Allowance for Bad Debts" account.

Accumulated Depreciation

There is also a contra-account for fixed assets, called "Accumulated Depreciation". When a fixed asset is purchased, the purchase amount is recorded in a fixed asset account. For office furniture, purchases are usually recorded in an account called "Furniture and Fixtures". Office furniture is a "depreciable asset". Instead of being expensed at the time of purchase, depreciable assets are expensed over time, over a few years or over several years depending on the type of fixed asset. This expense is called "depreciation expense" and is usually debited to a depreciation expense account and credited to an "Accumulated Depreciation" account.

> ➤ Because it is often required and desirable to keep record of and to report the original purchase costs of fixed assets, depreciation expense entries are recorded in an "Accumulated Depreciation" account, that is a contra-account to fixed assets.

> ➤ Organizations usually have several fixed assets that have been purchased over time. When it is decided to retire, sell, or otherwise dispose of a fixed asset, then the particular fixed asset is written off out of the fixed asset record (credited), the particular fixed asset general ledger account is credited, and the accumulated depreciation account is debited. For example, a ten-year old desk is trashed and fully depreciated. In that scenario, a credit is made in the furniture and fixtures account for the cost of the desk, and the accumulated depreciation account is debited. The specific fixed asset record for the desk is also "retired" in the fixed asset subsidiary ledger. At the time of disposal, if the desk is not yet fully depreciated, the accumulated depreciation account is debited for life-to-date accumulated depreciation at the time of disposal, and the difference between the cost of the desk less the accumulated depreciation is debited to a "loss on disposal" expense account, assuming there is no money received upon the disposal.

> ➤ Because organizations usually have several fixed assets and different categories of fixed assets that have differing depreciation methods and life-spans, usually there is a subsidiary ledger for fixed assets like there is for accounts receivable.

> ➤ The net fixed assets balance is the sum of the balances in the fixed asset accounts less the sum of the balance(s) in the accumulated depreciation account(s). Often, there is one accumulated depreciation account. However, there can be more than one account.

There are several other asset types organizations need to account for in the general ledger. Though different asset types may have unique valuation and reporting requirements, the accounting mechanics are the same for each general ledger account. And for a few general ledger accounts, there may be a related subsidiary ledger or contra-account or both.

Liabilities

Generally, liabilities are amounts organizations owe to others, sometimes called obligations. Some examples are accounts payable, wages payable, other payroll liabilities, short-term debt, and long-term debt. The application of the accounting mechanics for liabilities is the same as it is for assets, except we are now on the right side of the accounting equation. Let's explore the application for accounts payable.

Accounts Payable

The accounts payable general ledger account is used to record the amounts owed to vendors for goods and services purchased from them to be paid later. Some goods and services might be purchased with a company credit card. However, it is common to purchase goods and services from vendors, and pay within the terms of payment, for example, within 30 days.

A few types of goods and services that are purchased are inventory, office supplies, landscaping services, cleaning services, office furniture, equipment, and consulting services. Let's say a company purchases $300 worth of office supplies from their office supply vendor. The company likely has a general ledger account named "Office Supplies Expense" or "Office Supplies". Once the purchase is made, the office supplies expense account is debited for $300 and the accounts payable account is credited for $300.

A business usually has several vendors. Therefore, there is a subsidiary ledger for accounts payable, similar to accounts receivable. Except with accounts payable, the individual accounts in the subsidiary ledger are "vendor" accounts. The accounts payable subsidiary ledger allows a business to know at any point in time, what it owes to each vendor and also know which vendors need to be paid in each payment cycle.

When a business pays a vendor, the vendor's account is debited, the accounts payable general ledger account is debited, and a cash account is credited.

There are many other types of liabilities organizations need to record and report, and there are separate general ledger accounts for those liabilities that are necessary or useful. Though the different types liabilities may have unique valuation and reporting requirements, the accounting mechanics are the same for each general ledger account.

Owners' Equity

Now let's explore Owners' Equity. Simply, owners' equity is the investment owners have contributed to the organization, plus the accumulated net income (or less the accumulated net loss) the organization has earned, less distributions to owners (equity withdrawals).

Owners' Capital

Owners' investments to a business are often called "Capital". The capital invested includes initial investments and subsequent additional investments. For one individual person starting a business (sole proprietor), usually the investment is from the owner's personal funds. Two or more individuals can form a business as a partnership. A partnership can also be two or more other businesses forming a new business. A person or a group can also organize as a corporation, or as a limited liability company (LLC). Each country has laws and regulations governing the type of organization structures that are allowed to operate a business.

The unique feature of a corporation is that owners are issued stock certificates that tell how many shares each owner has in the company. If a corporation is public and it is listed on a stock exchange (e.g., NY stock exchange, Nasdaq), then shares can be bought and sold by the general public amongst each other in the market, via third party firms and platforms that are registered and authorized to execute the transactions.

For a corporation, there is usually one account for each class type of stock issued to shareholders. These accounts are usually called "Capital Stock" with the stock class type also identified (e.g., common stock-voting, common stock-non-voting, preferred stock). It is also common for subsequent investments to be identified in a separate account called "Additional paid in Capital".

For other forms of organization (e.g., sole proprietor, partnership), each owner has their own equity account for the initial investment (e.g., Capital - Owner A) and any additional paid in capital.

Accumulated Net Income

The primary purpose of a business is to engage in activity with the public or other businesses, for which it was started, to generate income for the growth and continued existence of the business. Large businesses often have several lines of business or subsidiary companies. To get net income, businesses obtain revenue by selling goods and services. The revenues are offset by expenses the business has to incur and pay in order to get the revenue. If revenues are more than expenses, income is earned, called "net income". If revenues are less than expenses, it is called "net loss". Accumulated net income over the life of a business is a major component of owners' equity.

For corporations, there is a separate account for accumulated net income, it is called "Retained Earnings". For other forms of organization (e.g., sole proprietor, partnership), each owner's share of accumulated net income is included their respective owners' equity account (e.g., Capital - Owner A).

Distributions and Return of Capital

There are two types of payments to owners for return of equity. One is for a distribution of a portion or all of the net income. The other is for a return of capital.

For corporations, distributions of net income back to owners is called dividends. Dividends paid is a decrease in retained earnings. Sometimes, a contra-account called "Dividends" is setup where dividends are recorded. The net returned earnings is accumulated net income less accumulated dividends paid. In other forms of organization, distributions of net income are usually recorded in a "contra" owners' equity account called "Distributions" (e.g., Distributions - Owner A). Net owners' equity is the balance in the owners' capital accounts (e.g., Capital - Owner A) less the balance in the owners' distribution accounts (e.g., Distributions - Owner A).

For corporations, return of capital withdrawals are primarily the business buying back shares from shareholders. In other forms of organization, an owner may take out a portion of the invested capital. Another example is one partner leaving the business and taking out all of their portion of the capital invested.

Net Income

Accumulated net income was earlier described as a major part of owners' equity. There can also be a net loss. For simplicity, accountants often say "net income" as a generic term for both net income and net loss. Net income is simply net revenues minus net expenses.

Revenues and Expenses

Revenues are amounts received for goods or services that an organization sells or other types income (e.g., from investments). Expenses are amounts that an organization incurs in selling those goods or services and incurs in managing and operating the business.

Conceptually, revenues and expenses could be recorded directly into the owners' equity account or accounts. However, that is not useful or practical. For multiple reasons, businesses need to track revenues and expenses over defined time frames (monthly, quarterly, yearly). Therefore, revenues and expenses have their own accounts where transactions are recorded over a specified time frame, almost always yearly.

After the transactions are completed for the year, the revenue and expense accounts are cleared out and the net difference, net income or net loss, is recorded (closed) to an owners' equity account or accounts (Retained Earnings for corporations). Each revenue and expense account starts the new year with a zero balance.

In accounting textbooks, revenue and expense accounts are also defined as "temporary accounts" because of the closing out process. Conversely, in accounting textbooks, asset, liability, and equity accounts are defined as "permanent accounts" because they are not cleared out.

Accounting Mechanics for Revenues and Expenses

Using the two accounting rules, let's explore the accounting mechanics for revenues and expenses.

> ➢ In the big picture, remember that revenues and expenses are a component of owners' equity, even though they are temporarily tracked in separate accounts. And remember the accounting equation $A = L + E$.

> ➢ Given that revenues and expenses are part of owners' equity, both of them are on the right side of the accounting equation, included in E.

> ➢ Given that revenues increase owners' equity and owners' equity (E) is on the right side of the equation, and an increase on the right side in accounting means a credit, then an increase in revenue is a credit entry.

> ➢ Given that expenses decrease owners' equity and owners' equity (E) is on the right side of the equation, and a decrease on the right side is left, and left in accounting is a debit, then an expense is a debit entry.

> ➢ A more concise way of saying this is an increase in revenue increases owners' equity and is a credit. An increase in expense decreases owners' equity and is a debit.

> ➢ Likewise, a decrease in revenue decreases owners' equity and is a debit. A decrease in expense increases owners' equity and is a credit.

> ➢ To summarize: An increase on the right side is a credit and decrease on right side is a debit. E (owners' equity) is on the right side. Increase in revenue increases E (right side) and is a credit. Increase in expense decreases E (right side) and is a debit.

> ➢ Another way to summarize: Net Income equals Revenue (Increases E) less Expenses (decreases E). Positive net income increases E. Negative net income (net loss) decreases E. Increase in E is a credit. Decrease in E is a debit.

> ➤ All of this is the same result. Just saying it in different ways. Think of it in the way that best resonates with you.

Examples of revenue accounts are sales and sales returns (a contra-revenue). Examples of expense accounts are cost of sales, promotional expenses (e.g., advertising, promotions, digital marketing), fulfillment expenses (e.g., warehouse salaries, shipping), administrative expenses (e.g., administrative salaries, office supplies, utilities).

With a system of accounts for transactions, next there is a need for methods, procedures, and the mechanics for recording financial transactions into the accounts.

4. RECORDING FINANCIAL TRANSACTIONS

Each organization determines the specific methods, procedures, and mechanics for recording financial transactions. All of them include the following elements:

1. Identify the nature of the transaction and what is being received and what is being given up. It could be a simple transaction or it could be a multi-faceted transaction.

2. Determine the monetary value of each transaction component.

3. For each side of the transaction (what is being received and what is being given up), identify the general ledger account or accounts that the transaction components need to be recorded into. If there is a subsidiary ledger entry needed, identify the subsidiary ledger and the subsidiary ledger account (e.g., accounts payable subsidiary ledger, vendor account "xyz supplier").

4. Record the transaction, both the debit side(s) and the credit side(s) for the monetary values determined.

Transaction Journals

How are transactions recorded? Transactions are recorded in journals. Conceptually, transactions could be recorded directly into each account. However, for practical and efficiency reasons, transactions are recorded in journals, and the amounts are posted into the accounts from the journals.

The homes of transaction amounts are in the accounts. However, the journals are practical for ensuring the debits equal the credits for each transaction, before they are posted to the accounts. The journals also provide a useful audit trail when research is needed for a transaction. Examples of a few journal types are sales journal for sales, invoice journal for expenses, disbursements journal for payments, and the general journal.

The information recorded in a journal for a transaction will vary depending on the journal type. At a minimum, the data recorded in a journal will include:

- ➢ A unique identifier for the transaction, usually a journal number.

- ➢ Date

- ➢ Transaction description

- ➢ Account number

- ➢ Amount

On a general journal, all sides of the entry need to be entered. There might be separate columns for debit amounts and credit amounts. Or there might be one column for amounts. If there is one column for amounts, debits are entered as positive numbers and credits are entered as negative numbers.

On other types of journals, in modern accounting software, only one side of the entry may need to be entered. In this scenario, the software enters and posts the other side of the entry automatically, behind the scenes. In addition, for the one side that is entered, the account number might be included in the setup so that the user won't need to enter the account number.

In modern systems, there are data entry screens (e.g., online ordering, point-of-sale systems for stores, customer service) where data are entered first, and then posted to the journals from those data entry processes. Once transactions are entered in or posted to the journals, transactions are posted to the accounts from the journals, both the general ledger accounts and any applicable subsidiary ledger accounts. Since the primary focus of this book is the general ledger, let's further explore the general ledger account.

General Ledger Account

What does a general ledger account look like?

- ➢ Broadly, a general ledger account is a "place" or "home" where amounts with similar characteristics reside. For example, a cash account for the checking account at "ABC" bank contain the amounts of the cash portion of transactions going into and out of "ABC" bank checking account.

- ➢ Each account has a unique account number and has an account name.

➤ Each account can have both debit transactions and credit transactions. That is, there can be transactions that increase the account balance and transactions that decrease the account balance. For a cash account, which is an asset, remember that increasing an asset balance is a debit entry and decreasing an asset balance is a credit entry.

➤ Each account has a beginning balance, transactions that increase or decrease that balance, and an ending balance that can be calculated at any point in time.

➤ For each transaction in the account, a journal entry number is recorded, the transaction date is recorded, a short description of the transaction is recorded, the amount is recorded, and the identifier if it is a debit or credit (the identifier could be a debit column for debits and a credit column for credits, or it could be a positive number for debits and a negative number for credits).

General ledger account formats for displaying data

Whether from computer accounting systems, or from paper systems in the old days before computers, two common formats for displaying information from general ledger accounts are the traditional format and the modified traditional format. The traditional format includes:

➤ At the top in one row, are the account number followed by the account name.

➤ There are columns for journal entry number, date, description, debit amount, credit amount, and balance.

➤ On the first amount row is the date and the beginning balance.

➤ On the transaction lines are date, journal entry number, transaction description, amount of the transaction in the debit or credit column.

➤ The balance of the account. Some systems will display a running balance after each transaction and some systems will calculate the ending balance at the end of the time period, for example, at the end of a month.

The modified traditional format is the same as the traditional format except there is only one column for transaction amounts. Debits are displayed as positive numbers and credits are displayed as negative numbers.

Modern accounting systems allow expanded formats beyond the traditional formats. Accounting software and ERP systems that include a general ledger module allow the ability to have additional columns displayed for general ledger account transactions. For example, a reference to a source module of an entry and information from the source module (e.g., an entry from the accounts payable module may display the invoice number and vendor name).

There is an additional general ledger account format that is used for academic and instructional purposes, the "T" (Tee) account format. One or more "T" accounts are drawn with an elongated horizontal line at the top, and the account name, or its abbreviation, is written at the top. A description of the transaction is stated or written including example amounts, and the debit amounts and credit amounts are written in the appropriate named "T" accounts. Sometimes, a beginning balance, and a calculated ending balance is needed for the demonstration.

Trial Balance Reports

There are two types of trial balance reports. One report is a detailed trial balance for any particular general ledger account. The second report is a summary trial balance that lists all the general ledger accounts or a sub-set of the accounts and shows the summary balances of the accounts.

In modern accounting software and ERP systems, a report of any particular general ledger account, over a time frame, can be generated and displayed. This report is called a "detailed account trial balance". Usually, accountants will call it a "trial balance". The report will display information from the general ledger account in one of the formats described earlier. For example, let's assume a general ledger account for a checking account is assigned account number 1001 and is called "Cash - ABC bank". A detailed trial balance can be run for the cash account for the month of March 2023, that will show the March 1, 2023 balance, list the transactions for March 2023, and show the ending balance at March 31, 2023. A detailed account trial balance is useful in reconciling an account or for researching a question.

Sometimes it is useful to have a list of all the accounts and only their balances at a point in time, at the end of a year, for example. This report is called a "summary trial balance". Accountants will often also call this the abbreviated name "trial balance". The sum of all the balances in the general ledger accounts net to zero. That is, net debits equal net credits, the second accounting rule.

In a summary trial balance report, one popular format is one row for each account, that displays the account number, the account name, the beginning balance, the net debits, the net credits, a column that calculates the debits less the credits, and the ending balance. For example, for the month of March 2023, there is a column for the account number, account name, beginning balance at March 1, 2023, net debits for the month of March 2023, net credits for the month of March 2023, the difference of debits less credits, and the ending balance at March 31, 2023. There are also totals at the bottom of each amount column. The beginning balance column and the ending balance column each total to zero.

In modern times with accounting software, a summary trial balance of all the accounts is useful for reviewing overall balances of the accounts. Before computers and accounting software, when reports were done by hand, the summary trial balance of all the accounts was written by hand and it was the starting point for preparing financial reports.

5. FINANCIAL REPORTS

Each organization will have its own unique reporting requirements for internal and external purposes. There are internal reports to support operations, executive reports to support oversight and decision making, and there are reports that support regulatory reporting (e.g., income taxes, SEC filings, regulated industries). There are three common financial reports that almost all organizations generate at least once a year but most organizations generate more frequently (monthly, quarterly). The three common financial reports are the Balance Sheet, the Income Statement, and the Cash Flow Statement.

Balance Sheet

The Balance Sheet lists three major sections: Assets, Liabilities, and Owners' Equity. The amounts listed are the balances in the accounts at a specific point in time (e.g., at March 31, 2023).

> ➤ The assets section lists each asset's description and the balances in the accounts. Most often for clarity and readability, accounts are summarized into categories. For example, if there are six cash accounts, often, there is one line called "Cash and the sum of the balances in the six cash accounts is the amount listed next to "Cash" on the balance sheet. At the end of the asset section, a total of the assets is listed as "Total Assets". Usually, assets are also listed in sub-categories with sub-totals; for example, a sub-category called "Current Assets" (e.g., cash, accounts receivable, credit card receivable), a sub-category called "Fixed Assets" (e.g., Equipment, Furniture and Fixtures, Buildings, Accumulated Depreciation), a sub-category called Long-term Assets (e.g., long-term investments), and any other sub-category that may be useful.

> ➤ The liabilities section lists each liability description and the balances in the accounts. The sub-categories are usually "Current Liabilities" (e.g., accounts payable, payroll liabilities) and "Long-Term Liabilities" (e.g., long-term loans). At the end of the liabilities section, a total of the liabilities is listed as "Total Liabilities".

> ➢ The Owners' Equity section lists the Owner's equity components previously described and the balances in the accounts. It also lists the year-to-date total net income generated for the period ending at the balance sheet date. (e.g., at March 31, 2023). At the end of the owners' equity section, a total of the owners' equity is listed as "Total Owners' Equity".

> ➢ The last line of the balance sheet is listed as "Total Liabilities and Owners' Equity". This is the sum of total liabilities plus owner's equity, and equals the amount of "Total Assets"

Income Statement

The Income Statement lists two major sections: Revenues and Expenses. The amounts listed are over an extended time frame (e.g., for the month ended March 31, 2023; for the fiscal year ended March 31, 2023). Sometimes there are other sections, a common one is Other Income and Expenses (e.g., miscellaneous income, one-time uncommon expenses). There are usually sub-totals for major categories, for example, sales, cost of sales, promotional expenses, fulfilment expenses, and administrative expenses. The resulting difference at the end of the income statement is net income (or net loss).

> ➢ The revenue section lists the revenues earned over the time-frame represented on the income statement (e.g., sales revenue, service revenue). Each type of revenue may also list revenues by lines of business (e.g., consumer business; sales to other businesses) or may list revenues by any other category the business determines useful (e.g., by geographic region).

> ➢ The expense section lists the expenses incurred over the time-frame represented on the income statement (e.g., cost of sales, promotional expenses, fulfilment expenses, administrative expenses). These lines can be as summarized or as detailed as deemed useful or necessary all the way down to a specific general ledger account.

> ➢ The last line of the income statement is the resulting net income (or net loss). This is the calculation of revenues less expenses.

Cash Flow Statement

The Cash Flow Statement lists the beginning cash balance at the start of a balance sheet's time-frame (e.g., March 1, 2023), lists the change in cash during the time-frame of the income statement (e.g., for the month ending March 31, 2023), and lists the ending cash balance at the end of a balance sheet's time-frame (e.g., March 31, 2023).

➢ Beginning cash balance and ending cash balance say it all. They are the cash balances at the beginning time-frame of the cash flow statement and the cash balance at the end of the time-frame of the cash flow statement (e.g., March 1, 2023 and March 31, 2023)

➢ The change in cash is broken out by types of financial activity over the time-frame (e.g., for the month ending March 31, 2023). The types of activities are operating activities, funding activities (borrowing and owners' investments), and investment activities (buildings, equipment, investments, acquisitions).

   o Operating activities are the cash components of net income. This is net income from the income statement, then adding and subtracting changes in non-cash working capital (e.g., accounts receivable, accounts payable, inventory).

   o Funding activities are changes in long-term borrowing and changes in non-operating owners' equity. Examples of long-term borrowing activities are the issuing bonds or paying off bonds, taking out new long-term bank loans or paying off loans. Examples of changes in equity are the issuance of additional stock, buying back stock, dividend payments.

   o Investment activities are acquisitions or liquidations of long-term assets. Examples are purchasing or liquidating buildings and equipment. Other examples are an acquisition of another company, or purchasing and selling financial assets (e.g., stock in another company).

6. SUMMARY

Every organization needs to capture the financial impact of its activities in order to perform financial operations and to consistently measure and report how it is doing financially. Double entry accounting is the core system used to serve those purposes. The specific application will look different between industries and organizations. The specific programing and mechanics will look different in the various computer software systems. However, the conceptual basis of accounting is the same in all organizations and in all the software.

The basis is the simple math equation $c = a + b$. Accounting is an eloquent and intricate application of that equation. The accounting version is "Assets equal Liabilities plus Owners' Equity". Inherent in that equation is the left side of the equation equals the right side. In accounting terminology, "Debits equal Credits". In accounting, these are known and referred to as the "two accounting rules"

The primary elements of every accounting system are balanced financial records, a system of accounts, methods and procedures for recording financial transactions, and reporting financial results.

There is much more, volumes actually, to the subject of accounting than the basics presented in this book. These basics are the foundation to build on in additional reading and study.

ABOUT THE AUTHOR

David is a financial and accounting professional with over thirty-five years of experience in retail, higher education, telecommunications, and public accounting. The author has a B.S.-Accounting, M.S.-Accounting, and MBA degrees.

David's first exposure to accounting was in a bookkeeping 1 class as a junior in high school. As a senior, he enrolled in and completed the bookkeeping 2 class. David continued his accounting journey in college, majoring in accounting. His accounting journey continues at the time of this book's writing.

www.ingramcontent.com/pod-product-compliance
Lightning Source LLC
Chambersburg PA
CBHW060501200326
41520CB00017B/4871